FLORIDA'S VACATION LANDS

This edition published in 1992 by SMITHMARK Publishers Inc.,
112 Madison Avenue, New York, NY 10016
ISBN 0-8317-6955-6
Printed and bound in Hong Kong
Designer: Ann-Louise Lipman   *Writer:* Joan E. Ratajack
Production: Valerie Zars   *Photo Researcher:* Edward Douglas
Assistant Photo Researcher: Robert V. Hale
Editorial Assistant: Carol Raguso

Index of Photographers

All photographs courtesy of The Image Bank. For
information contact The Image Bank, 111 Fifth Avenue,
New York, NY 10003

Janeart Ltd. endpapers. *Michael Melford* 5. *Joseph Devenney* 8 Top, 20 Top. *Luis Castañeda* 8 Bottom, 10, 14. *Andy Caulfield* 9, 11, 12-13, 21. *Paul Trummer* 15, 22 Top. *Alfredo Tessi* 16 Top. *Jürgen Vogt* 16 Bottom, 19 Bottom, 26 Top. *Margarette Mead* 17. *Grant V. Faint* 18 Top, 27 Bottom. *Walter Iooss, Jr.* 18 Bottom. *Marvin E. Newman* 19 Top. *Patti McConville* 20 Bottom. *William Kennedy* 22 Bottom. *Bullaty/Lomeo* 23 Top. *David W. Hamilton* 23 Bottom. *Murray Alcosser* 24 Top. *George Obremski* 24 Bottom. *Gary Farber* 25. *Andrea Pistolesi* 26 Bottom. *Back From Abroad* 27 Top. *Marc Romanelli* 28. *Al Satterwhite* 29.

Title page: **The famous water-skiing
shows have been performed at
Cypress Gardens since the 1940's.**

INTRODUCTION

Known today as a refuge for frostbitten northerners or "snowbirds," Florida boasts a long history of attracting travelers. Even while a good portion of the earth was locked in its final ice age, Florida was a warm haven for the strange, prehistoric beasts whose remains form the bedrock of the land Juan Ponce de León claimed for Spain in 1513.

Spanish heritage is evident today in St. Augustine, the oldest city in the nation, where the Castillo de San Marco and the Mission of Nombre de Dios stand cheek by jowl with modern-day hotels and tourist attractions. But many other cultures have left their marks on this fascinating state. The thriving Little Havana section of Miami is home to many Cubans who fled the island that's only 90 miles from Key West, the southernmost point of the United States. The tiny sponge-fishing community of Tarpon Springs boasts a sizeable Greek population, while the descendants of Osceola's Seminoles still inhabit sections of Florida's mysterious "rivers of grass," the Everglades region.

Thanks to the hospitable climate and the warmth of the Floridians themselves, vacationers from everywhere are made to feel welcome on the miles of wide beaches, acres of forests, and thousands of rivers, streams, and lakes. Sports enthusiasts are drawn by baseball's spring training camps, exciting jai-alai matches, dozens of golf courses, hundreds of tennis courts, and the thrill of deep-sea fishing. Whether it is the human-built attractions of Walt Disney World, Sea World, or Busch Gardens, or the natural loveliness of sunset at Key West, the shells on the beaches of Sanibel and Captiva islands, or the exotic wildlife at Everglades National Park, Florida truly has something for everyone.

Above: These lions on St. Augustine's Bridge of Lions keep watch over the Matanzas River. *Below:* The Castillo de San Marco has been guarding St. Augustine for well over 300 years. *Opposite:* This statue commemorates Juan Ponce de León, who claimed Florida for Spain in 1513.

Left: The Basilica Cathedral of St. Augustine houses
records dating to 1594, the oldest written records
in the country. *Above:* Visitors to the Kennedy
Space Center stand in awe at the sight of a space
shuttle launch. *Overleaf:* A closer view shows
a rocket propelling the shuttle into space.

Main Street, U.S.A. is the site of
this charming City Hall, as well as
the popular Main Street
Electrical Parade.

© The Walt Disney Company

Cinderella's Castle soars 18 stories
above Walt Disney World's
Magic Kingdom.

Above: The largest marine-life park in the world, Sea World is home to thousands of species of marine animals. *Below:* Witnessing the underwater mermaid show is the highlight of a visit to Weeki Wachee. *Opposite:* Moss-draped cypress trees are just one of the sights along Florida's more than 1,000 miles of coast.

Above: The nation's seventh-largest port, Tampa boasts skyscrapers as well as the ubiquitous palm trees. *Below:* Many of baseball's major league teams hold their spring training in Florida and play exhibition games in March and April.

Above: Sarasota's John and Mabel Ringling Museum of Art houses a world-renowned baroque collection. *Below:* Colonnaded galleries front exquisite formal gardens at the museum.

Above: Although the Gulf Coast's Sanibel Island has tourist accomodations, the island is largely occupied by a wildlife refuge. *Below:* Fashionable Naples residents can catch a magnificent sunset from the pier. *Opposite:* Everglades National Park at the tip of Florida is home to these basking alligators.

Above: Key West's Captain Tony's draws Hemingway fans and revelers of all sorts.
Below: Islamorada, on Upper Matecombe Key, is the site of a sport fishing festival in February.

Above: Key West's Strand Theater was built in 1918 by Cuban artisans. *Below:* Dozens of cats inhabit this house where Ernest Hemingway wrote about 70 percent of his work.

Above: James Deering's extravagant villa, Vizcaya, boasts 34 rooms and formal gardens. *Below:* Built over 40 years by one man, Coral Castle has a stone rocking chair and a stone telescope. *Opposite:* Although not native to Florida, these bright parrots at Miami's Parrot Jungle flourish in the tropical climate.

Above: Visible from Collins Avenue, this mural on a wall of the Fontainebleu Hotel was designed by Richard Haas. *Below:* An exclusive condominium on Bricknell Avenue makes a whimsical statement.

Above: Miami's nighttime skyline rivals its daytime brilliance. *Below:* Miami Beach is famous for its many pastel, art deco hotels.

Above: The beach at Fort Lauderdale stands ready
to receive its yearly influx of "spring breakers."
Opposite: Dusk falls on Worth Avenue, ritzy
Palm Beach's famed shopping street.